@RosenTeenTalk

TIME MANAGEMENT

Amy B. Rogers

ROSEN PUBLISHING

Published in 2026 by The Rosen Publishing Group, Inc.
2544 Clinton Street, Buffalo, NY 14224

First Edition

Editor: Greg Roza
Designer: Michael Flynn

Photo Credits: Cover, pp. 3, 5, 45 Slatan/Shutterstock.com; cover (emoji) Cosmic_Design/Shutterstock.com; cover and interior (phone) Vitya_M/Shutterstock.com; pp. 3, 13 Dmytro Zinkevych /Shutterstock.com; pp. 3, 21 Daniel Hoz/Shutterstock.com. pp. 3, 31 BongkarnGraphic/Shutterstock.com; p. 6 ZeroBB/Shutterstock.com; p. 7 Prostock-studio/Shutterstock.com; p. 9 Nikita Burdenkov/Shutterstock.com; p. 10 LightField Studios/Shutterstock.com; p. 11 wavebreakmedia/Shutterstock.com; p. 14 pics five/Shutterstock.com; p. 15 Prostock-studio/Shutterstock.com; p. 17 Xavier Lorenzo/Shutterstock.com; p. 19 Motortion Films/Shutterstock.com; p. 20 Overearth/Shutterstock.com; p. 22 Robin Craig/Shutterstock.com; p. 23 AkuZone/Shutterstock.com; p. 25 hxdbzxy/Shutterstock.com; p. 27 Lokana/Shutterstock.com; p. 29 New Africa/Shutterstock.com; p. 33 Davor Geber/Shutterstock.com; p. 34 pics five/Shutterstock.com; p. 37 Ollyy/Shutterstock.com; p. 39 Vladimir Sukhachev/Shutterstock.com; p. 41 antoniodiaz/Shutterstock.com; p. 43 Rawpixel.com/Shutterstock.com;

Some of the images in this book illustrate individuals who are models. The depictions do not imply actual situations or events.

Cataloging-in-Publication Data

Names: Rogers, Amy B.
Title: Time management / Amy B. Rogers
Description: Buffalo, NY : Rosen Publishing, 2026. | Series: @RosenTeenTalk | Includes glossary and index.
Identifiers: ISBN 9781499479966 (pbk.) | ISBN 9781499479973 (library bound) | ISBN 9781499479980 (ebook)
Subjects: LCSH: Time management. | Self-management (Psychology)..
Classification: LCC BF637.T5 R64 2026 | DDC 155.419--dc23

Manufactured in the United States of America

CPSIA Compliance Information: Batch #CWRYA26. For Further Information contact Rosen Publishing at 1-800-237-9932.

CONTENTS

Chapter 1

What Is Time Management?

I hate school! I just can't keep up with all this homework! I was up past midnight yesterday trying to finish the essay for English. I didn't even get to the math homework! I fell asleep in second period Earth science.

Coach Thompson says I'm in danger of being kicked off the volleyball team if my grades keep sliding. Volleyball is about the only thing I like about school! I just don't know what to do. On top of all this, Dad wants me to think about getting a part-time job. I don't have time for that!

Derrick's problems with school may sound familiar to you. It's common for teens to feel overwhelmed with their daily workload.

WHAT WE'RE MAKING TIME FOR

With all the activities we need and want to do every day, fitting everything into 24 hours can be nearly impossible. No matter who you are and what you like to do, you've probably had to decide between two or more activities. Sometimes we pour so much time into one activity, we forget other activities. Sometimes we feel we have so much to do that we can't **focus** on any activity. This is when time-management skills can help.

DAILY DOINGS

- CHORES
- EXERCISE
- FAMILY
- FRIENDS
- MEALS
- MUSIC LESSONS
- PETS
- READING
- SCHOOL
- SLEEP
- SOCIAL MEDIA
- SPORTS
- TELEVISION
- WORK

Wow, that's a lot to think about!

WHY IS TIME MANAGEMENT IMPORTANT?

Time management is all about being organized. That may sound like a boring topic to discuss, but it's something everyone should understand. Time-management skills can help us be successful in all areas of life—school, work, sports, and more. Being organized and understanding time management helps us build a solid foundation (or base) to personal independence and future success.

Successfully managing our time allows us to make educated decisions about our lives and activities. It helps remove stress from our lives. Stress is a state of worry. It's a natural reaction that helps us identify and deal with challenges. However, stress can be a problem when it occurs a lot. Time management can help us feel more in control and less stressed out.

Homework can be a source of stress for teenagers. It takes up time that teens would rather spend doing other things.

DON'T FORGET FREE TIME!

It's also important to schedule leisure time, or free time. This is when we aren't working, going to school, sleeping, or doing chores. We use our free time for lots of reasons—gardening, video games, movies, hiking, and whatever else people like to do for pleasure.

LEARNING DISORDERS

Time management doesn't have to be a complex process. It's a skill many people learn as they grow up, go to school, and get a job. Sometimes it's just a matter of learning to focus on basic organizational skills. However, some have more trouble with time management. Some **learning disorders** can **interfere** with the ability to manage time properly. These include ADHD, dyslexia, and dysgraphia.

Growing Brains

The frontal lobe is the part of the brain that controls planning, memory, emotions, **impulse** control, and more. The teen brain isn't fully developed until about age 25.

Dyslexia is a condition of the brain that makes reading difficult. Dysgraphia is a brain condition that makes writing difficult.

WHAT IS ADHD?

Attention-deficit/hyperactivity disorder (ADHD) is a learning disorder that makes it hard to focus. Signs of ADHD include restlessness, poor impulse control, mood swings, trouble completing tasks, and trouble with planning. It first shows up in childhood and can last into adulthood. ADHD can be treated with medications and therapy.

Read more about ADHD and other learning disorders:

- **kidshealth.org/en/parents/adhd.html**
- **www.healthline.com/health/mental-health/learning-disabilities**

Chapter 2

TIME MISMANAGEMENT

Why might someone struggle with managing time effectively? It almost always comes down to a person's **habits**.

Exercise is an excellent daily habit. It helps us stay fit, it makes us feel good about ourselves, and it helps us get a good night's sleep. Skipping lunch to watch videos on social media, on the other hand, is a bad habit. It's a mismanagement of your time! There's got to be a way to fit both lunch and social media time into a daily **routine**.

It's a good idea to fit both exercise and lunch into your daily routine. You'll read more about good and bad time-management habits in Chapter 4.

PROCRASTINATION

Procrastination means putting projects off until the last minute. This is usually paired with feelings of stress or **anxiety**. This can happen for many reasons. Often, the person who is procrastinating lacks **motivation**. But waiting to feel motivated doesn't always happen. Someone may not feel they have enough time to complete a project, so they don't even try.

Procrastination can make doing homework even more stressful.

PERFECTIONISM

Perfectionism means setting unrealistically high standards for oneself. Perfectionists want to do everything flawlessly with little or no help. They often have good **self-discipline**. But they allow self-discipline to get in the way of making progress. When perfectionists get stuck on a project, they tend to ignore all other projects. This results in anxiety because they can't do everything themselves.

Perfectionism can result in frustration, or the feeling that your efforts just aren't good enough.

Math Problems

Amber's mom Dorothy heard her scream from her bedroom. "Darn it! I'll never finish this!"

Dorothy looked in on her daughter. "Everything OK, Amber?"

Amber sighed and slammed a textbook closed. "I've been working on these stupid trigonometry problems for hours and I still don't get it! I have other homework to do but this is bothering me so much I can't stop."

Dorothy put a hand on Amber's shoulder. "It's not worth getting this upset. The best thing you can do is put the math away and work on something you like."

"I guess you're right, Mom. I'm excited to start that novel for English. I'll get help in math class tomorrow."

Much like Amber, you don't need to suffer alone if you are feeling overwhelmed. Reach out to people who care.

INTERRUPTIONS AND DISTRACTIONS

Many things can interrupt our efforts at time management. Interruptions are part of everyday life. Dogs need to be walked. Dishes need to be washed. Friends will call and text. Some interruptions are worse than others. Things that interrupt our sleep schedules can result in tiredness and lack of focus. You can avoid some interruptions by planning ahead: schedule time to walk dogs, do dishes, and hang with friends.

INTERRUPTIONS

- CHORES
- PHONE CALLS
- TEXTS
- VISITORS
- PETS
- WEATHER EVENTS

Distractions are a kind of interruption. They include television, social media, video games, and even a window facing a busy street (look, a bird!). Distractions can be hard to control because we *want* to be distracted. We *want* to play video games and watch television, but those things stop us from being productive. It can be difficult to avoid distractions!

Interruptions and distractions can be frustrating. They stop us from getting things done on time.

DISTRACTIONS

- **VIDEO GAMES**
- **TELEVISION**
- **INTERNET**
- **MUNCHIES**
- **TEXTING**
- **TOYS**

Chapter 3

SCHEDULING POWER

Sometimes it's hard to fit everything we want and need to do into 24 hours. At least eight of those hours need to be spent asleep for our health. School takes up another seven or eight hours, without counting **extracurricular** activities. Some teens have a job that eats away more time.

It can be stressful when daily tasks build up. It can be hard to choose what to do first, making it hard to even get started. This is when creating a schedule can help.

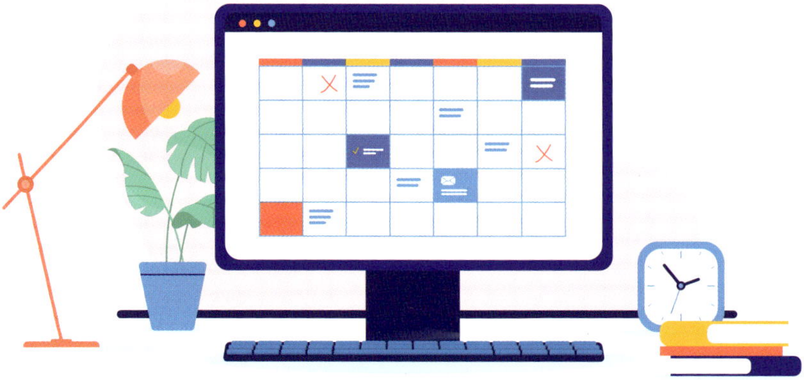

Scheduling helps us organize our thoughts about our priorities, or the things we need to do. Scheduling helps us plan for reachable goals.

PRIORITIZING

A priority is an activity or event that's more important or **urgent** than others. Prioritizing means placing activities in order of importance. Let's say your friend wants to see a movie, but your dad wants you to mow the lawn. Which activity should be a priority? Your dad would mostly likely want you to mow the lawn before going to the movies. Your friend may disagree. But you need to decide which is more important.

Listing is the first step when prioritizing. Then ask yourself: Which tasks are very important and which are less important? Which tasks are urgent and which are less urgent? By answering these questions you can start to place tasks in order of importance—or prioritize them.

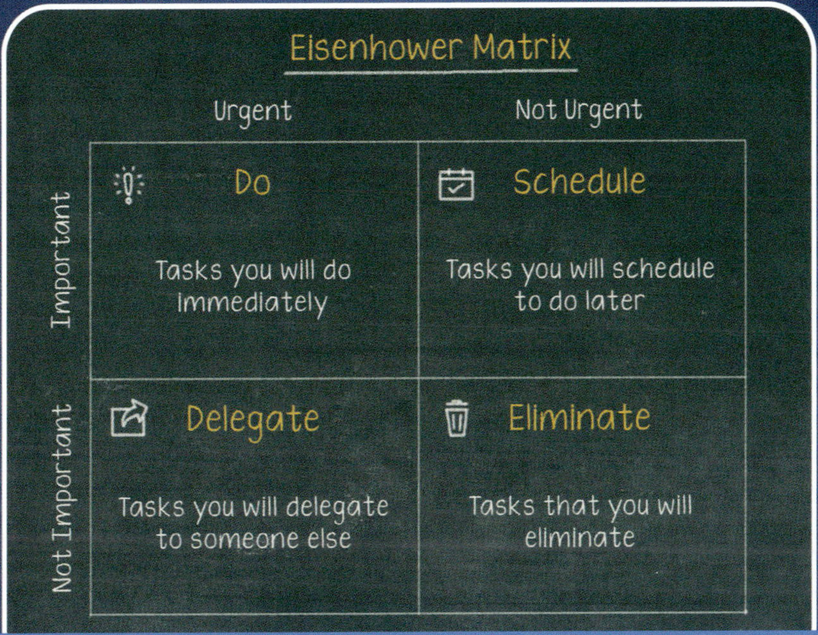

You can read more about the Eisenhower matrix here: **productivitypatrol.com/eisenhower-matrix**

THE EISENHOWER MATRIX

U.S. President Dwight D. Eisenhower was very organized and productive. The graphic, or **matrix**, above was created to explain his beliefs about time management.

SETTING GOALS

Once you know what your priorities are, it's time to set goals. A goal is the final result you're hoping to reach. Examples of goals include learning to play piano, getting a raise at work, saving up to buy a new smartphone, and finishing a marathon. Some goals are bigger or more important than others. For example, you might need to get a raise at work before you can think about buying a new phone.

Setting a huge goal, such as graduating high school, can seem scary! That's when smaller goals can help. Smaller goals are like stones in a stream. You can't just jump from one side of the stream to the other. But you can use the stones to make it across one step at a time. For the main goal of "travel the world," smaller goals may include getting a job, saving money, reading about world cultures, and learning a new language.

Reaching smaller goals helps us feel a sense of accomplishment (getting things done). This motivates us to keep moving on to the next goal.

TECHNIQUES AND TOOLS

Prioritizing, setting goals, and managing your time effectively are skills anyone can learn. Some techniques, or methods, can help you be successful. When creating a schedule, it is helpful to use blocks of time. For instance, if you're more productive in the afternoon, the morning block of time could be used for easier tasks. Then, plan an afternoon block of time for more difficult activities.

Knowing how to create a budget will also help. A budget is a plan for how to use money. Budgets help us keep track of the money we have, what we want to spend, and what we want to save. This skill can be used to create a time budget—how much time do you have, how much time can you spare, and how much time does that leave you for personal time?

TIME-MANAGEMENT TOOLS

- NOTEBOOK/PAPER
- PENS
- PLANNER
- SMARTPHONE APPS
- TIMERS AND ALARMS
- YOUR BRAIN!

Using different colors when creating a schedule can help you organize your time better.

ON-THE-GO!

There are many time-management apps for smartphones. Many of them are free. It can help to have an organizer in your pocket wherever you go! Do some research to find the best one for you.

WHAT IS BULLET JOURNALING?

Maintaining a schedule may not sound very exciting to everyone. Bullet journaling is a fun way to make the scheduling process more personal, enjoyable, and effective. A bullet journal is a planner you create with a blank notebook. It can be as simple or as detailed as you want.

Bullet journaling takes **patience** and careful planning. You may need to take an hour or two to set up your journal before the start of the week or month. But that's why bullet journaling is so effective. The extra time you spend thinking about, writing about, and reading about your priorities and goals, the easier you will remember them.

More Info

Read more about bullet journaling here:

- **www.theintentionalmom.com/bullet-journaling-for-teens-written-by-a-teen**
- **bulletplannerideas.com/what-should-a-teen-put-in-a-bullet-journal**

You can make a bullet journal that's simple and straightforward. You can make it detailed and colorful. No matter what your style is, a bullet journal can help manage your time!

TIPS FOR BULLET JOURNALING

- Any notebook will work.
- Black ink helps writing stand out.
- Markers and highlighters help add color.
- A ruler will help you draw neat lines.
- Stickers can add **flair**!
- Jot down things you want to remember: books you want to read, pet names, recipes, favorite quotes…whatever you want!

Chapter 4

Mastering Time Management

My friend Karl is always so organized. It's kind of annoying! But it sure helps him stay on top of things. Today in study hall he noticed that I was stressed out and asked if I was OK.

"I'm just so overwhelmed right now." I said. "I've got so much to do and I can't even find time to finish the dress I'm trying to make for the winter dance. I probably won't go."

"What!? You gotta go, Lara! Listen, maybe I can help you with your workload and give you plenty of time to finish that dress."

"What do you mean, like, do my work for me?"

Karl laughed. "No! But I can teach you a bunch of time-management skills. If they work for me I'm sure they will work for you too."

"Well," I said, "That beats missing the dance!"

Reaching out to others in need is always a good thing. Maybe, after reading this book, you can help someone else master time management too!

PERSONAL STOCKTAKING

Personal stocktaking means reflecting on (thinking about) your strengths, weaknesses, and values. It's an ongoing process. Thinking about your strengths and weaknesses helps you identify bad habits, which is the first step in getting rid of them. It also helps you identify good habits.

You can start stocktaking by reflecting on daily events at the end of the day. *Which activities went well? Which activities had problems?* The answers will help you adjust your work methods to be more effective. In turn, this can help you manage your time and reduce stress caused by the process.

In the business and manufacturing world, stocktaking means counting and recording the amount of goods, or stock, that a business has.

GETTING TO KNOW YOURSELF

Stocktaking helps you gain a better understanding of yourself and your personal style. Here are some ideas to consider to begin stocktaking.

- What are my strengths? What are my weaknesses?
- What accomplishments am I proud of?
- What skills could I get better at?
- What goals can I set for myself for the coming week? Month? Year?

GOOD AND BAD HABITS

Once you've identified your strengths and weaknesses, you can apply that knowledge to your daily habits. Focus on improving good habits while avoiding bad habits.

Learning good time management habits and avoiding bad habits will help you feel more in control and less stressed.

DON'T DO THIS...	...DO THIS
Just start working, and you'll find out what you're doing as you go.	Set clear goals. Set smaller goals to break up bigger tasks.
Once you start working, don't stop for anything!	Work in blocks of time and take short breaks to stretch and drink water.
Alphabetize your tasks and get started at the top of the list.	Prioritize tasks from the most important and urgent to the least important.
Work on several tasks at once to get everything done.	Focus on a single task to improve productivity.
Eat lunch while you're working.	Take a break for lunch and enjoy a podcast or read a book.
Keep working on a task no matter how frustrating it is.	Take a break and focus on a different task. Come back to the first task after you've had time to think about it.
Keep a running list of tasks in your mind.	Create a schedule for the day and week so you can better understand your workload. This will help you prioritize tasks.
Put the television on while working.	Avoid distractions such as television, social media, and video games. Schedule breaks to do these things.

DEALING WITH DISTRACTIONS

Distractions are a huge problem for effective time management. You can build good habits to make it easier to avoid them. The best thing to do is to select a distraction-free zone, or area, where you can concentrate without interruption. This could be your kitchen or dining room table. Or it could be the local library.

DISTRACTION REACTION

- Create a zone that has limited distractions.
- Set specific times for work and breaks.
- Turn social media notifications off.
- Let people know that you need some time to yourself.
- Organize your desk or work area and hide or remove distractions.
- Practice mindfulness techniques (turn the page to learn more).

Many teens prefer to work in their bedroom. However, that's a bad idea if your room is filled with your favorite distractions! It's better to work in a place different from where you relax.

SCHEDULING DISTRACTIONS

One of the best ways to avoid distractions is to schedule them along with your work or homework. After an hour of work, take a 20-minute break to do a crossword puzzle, play a video game, or check on social media. When you schedule time for distractions, they're less likely to disrupt your work.

I'M OVERWHELMED!

Teens and adults alike can become overwhelmed with daily life. Time-management skills can help you cope with a busy schedule and overlapping **deadlines**. Scheduling time for breaks and distractions is a good start. It also helps to break single, large tasks into smaller, more manageable tasks.

WHAT IS MINDFULNESS?

Mindfulness is the practice of using the senses to be "fully present" in an activity. This means the mind is fully focused on where it is and what it's doing without being distracted by other thoughts. Instead of allowing our thoughts to complicate an issue, mindfulness keeps your brain focused. Mindfulness practices are incredibly helpful for many reasons. They can help you feel calm when you are stressed or overwhelmed.

Learn more about mindfulness here.

- **www.mindfulnessforteens.com**
- **anxiety-gone.com/mindfulness-activities-for-teens**

Daily exercise helps us stay fit. It gives us a chance to step away from work for a bit. It also helps reduce feelings of stress and anxiety.

ASK YOUR DOCTOR

Some conditions, such as ADHD and other learning disabilities, can cause people to feel overwhelmed frequently. Mindfulness helps! However, a doctor may also prescribe a medication to help. It's important to discuss these topics with your doctor before taking any medications.

GETTING MOTIVATED

There will be times when you just don't feel like doing what you need to do. It can be hard to stay motivated 100 percent of the time. Here is a list of advice that can help you stay focused and avoid procrastination.

Get organized: Cleaning up your workspace and getting rid of clutter helps you feel more productive.

Remove distractions: Put your phone in another room. Close the door to your room. Turn off the television.

Be positive: Don't be hard on yourself for lacking motivation. Think of your strengths and how they can help. Celebrate small successes.

Don't take on too much: A consistently full workload can wear you down. Sometimes you need to reduce your daily routine.

Break down large tasks: Hitting smaller goals gives you a sense of accomplishment.

Ask for help when needed: Parents, friends, teachers, and others might be able to help you work through a tough task.

Basketball legend Michael Jordan once said: "If you run into a wall, don't turn around and give up. Figure out how to climb it."

Chapter 5

FINDING BALANCE

Living a balanced life means that the different areas of your life are equally stable. This includes health, school, work, relationships, and more. It can be challenging to keep all these areas in balance. It requires patience and self-discipline. The advice in this book is meant to help you become more organized. It will help you to maintain clear, focused thinking. It will show how to adjust your methods and strategies to produce better results.

Time management is a set of skills anyone can learn. It just takes some practice! Mastering time management can bring balance to your life.

Time management is a skill all people can learn and master. You may even help friends with becoming time management masters!

Derrick's Success

My grades were getting so bad that the school counselor, Mrs. Vance, asked to talk to me. I'm so glad she reached out! She showed me how helpful time-management skills can be. She showed me how to make a daily planner and to-do lists. She showed me how to balance all my homework, practice, and free time! I never thought that was possible. I might even get a part-time job!

Now, my grades are picking up. I got an A+ on my history report. Coach Thompson even gave me a high-five when he saw me today. Time management saved me!

Much like Derrick, you don't need to suffer alone if you are feeling overwhelmed. Reach out to people who care.

GLOSSARY

anxiety: Fear or nervousness about what might happen.

deadlines: A date or time before which something must be done.

extracurricular: Relating to school activities that aren't part of a course of study.

flair: An eye-catching decoration.

focus: Uninterrupted concentration.

habit: An activity that is repeated over many days, weeks, or months.

impulse: A quick feeling or desire to take action.

interfere: Get in the way of.

learning disorder: A condition of the brain that makes learning difficult.

maintain: To keep something in a positive state.

matrix: A grid or framework used to make comparisons and decisions.

motivation: The feeling of wanting to get something done.

patience: The ability to stay calm in spite of delays and struggles.

routine: A regular way of doing things in a particular order.

self-discipline: The ability to make yourself do things that should be done.

urgent: Requiring immediate attention.

INDEX